We Are Chimera

We Are Chimera

Poems by

Laura Sobbott Ross

© 2025 Laura Sobbott Ross. All rights reserved.
This material may not be reproduced in any form, published,
reprinted, recorded, performed, broadcast,
rewritten or redistributed without
the explicit permission of Laura Sobbott Ross.
All such actions are strictly prohibited by law.

Cover design by Shay Culligan
Cover art by Romilda Bozzetti

ISBN: 978-1-63980-768-0

Kelsay Books
502 South 1040 East, A-119
American Fork, Utah 84003
Kelsaybooks.com

*. . . women carry at least three unique cell populations
in their bodies—their own, their mother's, and their child's—
creating what biologists term a microchimera . . .*

—Katharine Rowland

Acknowledgments

I'm grateful to the editors of the following publications in which these poems first appeared, some in different form:

Asylum Magazine: "Baker Acted"
Autumn Sky Poetry: "Time Zones"
The Bedford Competition 2022: Finalist, "When Your Jamaican Grandmother Sings to You"; Semi-finalist, "Year of the Turtle"
Crosswinds Poetry Journal: "She Who Begat Her Who Begat Her"
Illya's Honey: "An Egg Inside of an Egg Inside of an Egg"
Main Street Rag: "Ultrasound"
Mande: "Purge," "Pink Chords"
National Poetry Review: "Amaryllis"
Off the Coast: "Each, a Fossil of Finer Urgencies"
Turtle Way: "Pears, the Same Shape as Tears"
Wilderness House Literary Review: "We Are Chimera"
Yalobusha Review: "Come to Where I Live, She Says"

Two poems were first published in chapbooks:

My Mississippi (Anchor & Plume Press): "An Egg Inside of an Egg Inside of an Egg"

To the Patron Saint of Wayward Daughters (Kelsay Books, 2021): "Concordance"

Much appreciation to John Hughes, Dan Sobbott, and Sharlyn Page for feedback on this manuscript, and to Lynne Davis Spies for your thoughtful editing and your encouragement! Thank you so much to Kelsey Books for taking this journey with me again. Much love to my son and daughter who hone and own my mother-heart. "Ultrasound" is dedicated to the memory of Bernie Welch.

Contents

We Are Chimera	11
An Egg Inside of an Egg Inside of an Egg	13
Concordance	14
Divination Using a Mirror	16
Pears, the Same Shape as Tears	17
Purge	18
Russian Nesting Dolls	20
Pink Chords	21
Baker Acted	23
Myrna Faye	25
Year of the Turtle	27
Ultrasound	29
Hail Mary, Full of Grace	30
Wedding Day	31
Amaryllis	33
Hope Sheds in Layers Like a Flower	34
When Your Jamaican Grandmother Sings to You	36
Time Zones	38
Nocturnal, the Dark and Squirming	42
Come to Where I Live, She Says	43
Each, a Fossil of Finer Urgencies	45
Namesake	46
She Who Begat Her Who Begat Her	47

We Are Chimera

Did you know we exchange cells?
A fistful of your stardust settling
in the dark alcoves of my organs,
swirling up the channel of my spine.
My sweet mitochondrial, a mother's own
DNA, you'll share yours, too—
a sliver of Eve and the apple,
Adam's atoms clinging like a fig leaf.

Let go, daughter? Give up on you?
Tell that to the sticky web of my veins,
to the wishbone at my core you snapped
like a river current. Floating away
is what the clouds do, manifesting
into the sky. Girl in a flowered room,
I pondered you into being. Lit the candles.
Waited. Offered my marrow for your breath.

Still slippery, you were once small enough
to be caught by a midwife.
Newborn eyes slick as mercury,
your heartbeat and mine strung by a living cord.
Once it was cut, I was milk. Until I wasn't.

Years later, I have to ask: where do you go?
Even that sliver of moon
beneath which you disappear
is whole, an alchemy of shared light.
Softly threaded in is how I remember you—
my ankles, his earlobes, and a new rhythm
waking to the walls of our rooms.
Teething on lullabies, you grew hungry.
Even now, I can still hear you wail.

An Egg Inside of an Egg Inside of an Egg

We are women unfolded from one to another,
heartbeats catching a rhythm
through decades that flower and fade
into the quiet earth of our bones.

She who begat her who begat her.
Wouldn't we know the same constellations,
the purpled womb spreading open like a bloom,
the sick babies, the whiskered fever of men?

My grandmother's hands at the rim of a bowl,
snapped string beans like an art—
every pod broken into wholeness
meant a singular thread giving way,
while the bayou lay sleeping
in its mossy, swaying brim.

I remember the cry of peacocks
near her house on summer nights—
slender throated birds hoisting a multitude
of iridescent eyes through darkness.

The sun is a simple circle, my daughter shrugs
as if it were not important enough for her
to draw in the corner of her paper sky,
as if every absolute were not
just a simple circle in the universe—

a spring, a dawn, a seed, a cocoon,
a baby girl curled within a womb—
an egg inside of an egg inside of an egg

Concordance

I first saw you in the soundwaves—
echoes sketching your nested bones.
Hadn't I prayed a rosary across each
buoy of your spine, your whorled
fingertips chalked in the amnion?

Out of the womb, you were wild in the sea.
Sign of the fish, you delighted in the brokenness
of the tide; its buoyant salt, an equilibrium
offering flight, tumbling buried things
into new hidden places. You loved seeds
and cocoons and homeless creatures
with shiny eyes and fangs. The natural world,
a simple hunger. Not like reading
the same primers the way the other students did,
or how you wrote in mirror images,
gleaning currents through an inverted lens.

You don't like to draw anymore—
the crayoned lines of your childhood
plucked into a bitter cantata, jawed down
to hard wax notes of indigo and aquamarine.
Even the word *sorrow* sounds like a color,
full of gristle and floodwater. Looking back,

I was wide-eyed the first time
the jellied wand found you curled
and hiccupping inside your little cove,
the whole horizon tilted to catch
your flickering heartbeat.
Still, I wonder, what did I miss?

The technician's room lit
with the diorama of the ultrasound
while I lay belly up, parsing
the rudiments like tea leaves—
interpretation of a grainy concordance,
daughter, that could have been
you, that could have been me.

Divination Using a Mirror

You avoided sidewalk cracks.
Those long shinbones of yours,
buoyant, mapping out cadences,
childhood incantations on your tongue.

Mother and daughter, we were tangled—
knots I'd tried to smooth out in the teeth
of my comb. Hanging on by a hair,
you were already leaping

toward the neighborhood girls
who had a new game. You know the one
where you light a candle in a windowless room,
then take turns standing in front of a mirror
while you chant: *Bloody Mary, I've got your baby,*
Bloody Mary, I've got your baby,
Bloody Mary, I've got your baby,
till the shadows efface the image on the glass
into someone unrecognizable.

Pears, the Same Shape as Tears

Tears, as in crying,
    not to be confused with tears—
    places split in something soft.
        I'm remembering an old autumn
hardening like winter inside my teenage limbs.

Under a tree in the backyard,
    I'd released my sadness in salty heaves.
        Pears fell.
   They were mealy, blighted.
          No one bothered to pick them up.
Wasps dizzied themselves on fermenting flesh,
        buzzing with a sweet rot.

The red maple outside my window sharing my veins.
      Umbilicus, a word too clinical
      for what is given and what is taken
         from one body to another.

The scent of pears was where it started.
      The sadness, I mean.
          Daughter, forgive me

the gene pool, concise and flat as a mirror.
If only I could wipe the sticky fruit from your fingers,
    comb the wasps out of your hair.

Purge

I. Cutting

I think I can understand
the need for darkness
to howl open into a wound.
Better yet, the equilibrium
in someone else's wide-eyed recoil:
What have you done to yourself?
Your skin, a soft palette
beneath which you've hardened.
A canvas of deft strokes razored in red.
Nettles sting my tongue
when I try to speak about it.
Gauze, a flimsy construct
between your room and the hospital
that terrible night we got the call
from your landlord. Your skin
slashed with the same voracity
as the dashboard weeks before
when we took back your car.
Letters whose blunt strokes ran
intersections—*Fuck you.*
And it's what I thought at red lights
when I realized strangers
might be watching me cry.

II. January Super Blood Wolf Moon

Purge. It's been said about this
particular lunar energy—
Bald magnet, who could miss it,
red and heaving the tides.
My back is swept with shingles—
a word that feels barnacled,
as if I was a pier footing, a stinging
hull, a husk in the shape of a woman
in her window looking up.
Stupid January super blood wolf moon.
If only it was fiction—these things
my daughter is telling me, terrible things
she's rocked and tended inside
her ribcage, hinged and swinging wide.
Her words, a coil of ash,
like one of those black snake fireworks
that just keeps writhing out, volumetric
slag ribbon expanding against a red moon
held like the smoldering tip of a match.
She speaks and speaks, and I arc and char.

Russian Nesting Dolls

The wounded can't tell you anything about pain,
as if it was rooted in the skull like a molar.
There is no cartographer to map the psyche,
its dark fairytale forests and breadcrumb trails.
Have you ever uncapped those Russian nesting dolls

with the hope of finding something more than a girl
marrowed within a girl marrowed within a girl?
Shiny-eyed archetypes with smiles sealed in lacquer.
Each, a guardian of the next. An echo growing fainter.
Remember, princesses,

when you show up at the castle with storm raked hair,
and sleep fitfully because a single pea is a hidden inquest
beneath a stack of borrowed mattresses, remember,
pain can't always be pinpointed, unshelled, or shaken out
like a mother-bead, sacred and wrung thin with prayer.

You'll wake to puddles silvered and pieced
like a broken compass among wolf-shaped shadows.
If that pebble, still in your fingers, breaks the skin
between you & your reflection, you'll find nothing
but a circle opening inside a circle opening inside a circle.

Pink Chords

*Possessed by it, they rush off, whirl madly in circles,
or stand still, as if turned to stone*
—Walter F. Otto, *Dionysus: Myth and Cult*

You live in a rowhouse downtown
where you say there's voodoo and mold.
The Lord's Prayer hangs in a frame by the door.

People move as if underwater here.
The neighborhood, a fluorescent grid
buzzing and nettled in moths,
the collective croon of places where nothing
bigger than a twenty-dollar bill stays in the drawer
of a cash register, and pasties are the standard
issue of decorum for chiding expanses of skin.

You sleep while the sun levitates,
bitter and dreamless. Bruised, feeding on
smoke rings, you'll remember none of it.
I keep a broken piece of your girlhood,
warm beneath my sternum, where it lies sacred,
a relic offered in petition to the saints.

Despise sounds like a plateau, don't you think?
A natural habitat for skittish, wild things,
and not a word a girl would use against herself—
the chafing bones, the abiding taste of iron in her
throat. Didn't I knit you whole in small stitches—
jangling needles and pink chords, a consortium
of soft lies? Sometimes I think about the cat—

a calico you'd loved and released to the trance
inside its own girl-cells. Wary and left
to skulk oily puddles, kibble of glass and flint.
Moon throbbing like a car alarm.

Not fixed, you might say about the calico,
meaning the unaltered state that opens
one into another and another,
each strung on a sticky thread of afterbirth.
Pink fanged mouths poised in the night to suckle.
Their small, winded bodies, soft as warm bread.

Baker Acted

sounds like something risen,
dusted in powdered sugar.
At the least, a caramelized edge.
Rage coming off you like heat.

Diagnosis, a label needled in like a tattoo.
Another in an inked torso of comorbidities.
Your roommate telling you she is Hitler's wife
while she hisses at your attempts to pray.

On your pillow, you think: Surrender?
Which way? You are a compass recalibrating,
a spinning needle, a magnetic shift
beneath a storm weary sky. This time

you said you'd jump, got drunk on Campari
and spent the night in a hotel room
with a strange man. By that, I mean
risk. Impulsivity. Panic. Suicidal ideation.

All mapped in a universe that's pronged
and reads like order, if by order
you mean riddles that ease into riddles
because chaos is no blank slate,

and you're still an artist. Never mind
that they've taken away all sharp edges,
anything that can be used as a tool,
a stylus, a charcoal point, a wand

of lipstick in angel pink. Don't they know
you can't be broken if you're still
in midair? Mother cord in me, strung
and spooling. Do you have soap?

Warm socks? In a day or two,
someone will ask you for a signature.
The weather moving on the other side
of the wired glass suddenly back

on your tongue. You'll call
those you cursed on your way in,
or the one who left the bruises,
to pick you up and take you back.

Myrna Faye

written on a roadside memorial sign

Yours must be the name of the patron saint
of blind turns and falling trees,
of girls who are distracted.
You'd had a name like a flapper,
and I'm guessing you were a midwife.
All those aching mothers, steerage
in your hands. *Breathe through it,*
you must have coaxed,
conspirator of soft skull plates,
networker of pelvic bones.

Your name is anchored in silk
daffodils by a curve in the road
where my daughter rolled a car.
Her molars rattled
of their mercury fillings,
the night gone upside down
with your name written
across it like a benediction
Too drunk for a seatbelt,
she asked me later if rum
would help her concussion.

Bless you, Myrna Faye.
I bet you curled your ribbons
with the blade of a knife,
kept a lemon cake in the freezer,
and spades was your lucky suit.
Now your premonitions screech
into prayers. Speaking of which,

I'd had a dream about a baby girl
lifted from a collision
the way a newborn is held up
in a hospital delivery room—
that first breath, an altar.
God, she was perfect, picked clean
from the wreckage and wailing.

Year of the Turtle

It started when I found out you were pregnant,
deciphered it from a code on an insurance bill
after you'd taken a test at the emergency room.
But this is about turtles, isn't it?

Days later, turtles swam to your father and me
from the aqua shallows of the Caribbean,
their beaked mouths opening for bits of flesh—
not ours, but the light on the water
was winking and wickedly bright.

We brought home t-shirts. Purple
and turtled, the one for the baby's father
before we knew about his aquarium,
where turtles basked in a warm cone of light
and swallowed fish drifting like butterflies.

Then there was the cable man.
Cleverturtle is your new password,
he said just before we found
a turtle in the laundry room,
fleeced in dryer lint when you
and your new husband moved in.

A house within a house. A dole
of turtles patterning your pillows.
Dole, the collective, a word that means
something portioned, or sorrow
and grief. A breakup, I'd predicted.

But let's stick to actual interpretations
of turtles in dreams, as spirit animals,
and what can be discerned from patterns
of geometry in bone plates of shell—

good fortune, long life, spiritual protection
for the yet-to-be-born baby girl who is both
aquatic and terrestrial, black and white,
apprehension and hope.

Ultrasound

Constructed in echoes,
your ears, your lungs, your wrists.
We watch, aquarium close
as you are tweezered from the shadows,
a miraculous little current,
the color of fossil and pulp,
symbiotic with the earth
of your mother's flesh.
You fledge, hidden from this
barking dimension of light
that will clap you out, eye you over,
and groom you in alms
of flannel and milk. Trinkets
of lullaby waiting to be sprung
in a soft, readied room.
But in this momentary stasis
of our awe, we will only know
you as a quake, a hive, a balm
of all our marrows sipped from a jar-
ring communion of hope and breath.
Your swimmy ribs, the hollow of a shell.
Its soft creature heart, a juju
that shushes the room, nudges
open thresholds of window and door,
and releases its rhythm across the horizon,
rearranging everything.

Hail Mary, Full of Grace

Hail Mary, full of grace
   Mother to mother, thread my heart to yours
The Lord is with thee
   I couldn't sleep again last night
Blessed art thou among women
   Please pray for her, over her, with her
And blessed is the fruit of thy womb, Jesus
   I saw her face in the sound waves
Holy Mary, Mother of God
   I saw her face in a mugshot, broken in a hospital room
Pray for us sinners now
   What if, what if, what if, what if
And in the hour of our death
   Forgive me my own circulating chant, a wicked trance

Hail Mary, full of grace
   Do I dare to love this much?
The Lord is with thee
   To hope?
Blessed art thou among women
   Mother, pray she comes out untroubled
And blessed is the fruit of thy womb, Jesus
   Uncompromised by the shifting bedrock of strife
Holy Mary, Mother of God
   Nothing karmic or predisposed, nothing wounded
Pray for us sinners now
   Let her be a praise song, a girl-story rocked and lullabied
And in the hour of our death
   Beneath a holy relic in the shape of the moon

Wedding Day

October, and the cypress trees
were origami-ed in white ibises.
As if on cue, they unleafed,
floated by in a cloud.

We held our breath.
The groom, braided,
earnest in purple,
and the baby, almost

hidden in the flocked cottons
of your wedding skirt.
Orange canna lilies leaned
into the windows

of the Caribbean church,
where the pastor laid hands
on your heads, his voice
sealing you in scripture.

On your cake, *Lignum Vitae,*
not a benediction in Latin,
but a cluster of purple blossoms
native to Jamaica.

Wood of the tree,
hardest and heaviest in existence.
Its petals and resins,
a cure for everything

from hangnails to infertility to mania.
The cake beneath the fondant
was blood-red. You fed each other
mindfully in slivers.

Amaryllis

We readied the bulbs in the days before
the baby arrived. Full solstice moon
nudging what was curled inside its own
winter sleep, every bulb nested & rooting.
Miraculous, the way green startled
out, ribboned toward the light—
light that was a new dominion
lording across a tracery of capillaries,
eyelashes, flutter of breath,
the fusing of the soft crown of bone.
I'm talking about the baby,
of course, whose wails shuddered open
from her newly dredged lungs, while amaryllis
pushed and pushed its flame points skyward
till they fell over on their new, floppy necks
into the full-throated red of bell-shaped blossoms.

Hope Sheds in Layers Like a Flower

Okay, so, maybe it isn't that bad—
your lies and infidelity. The rages.
The impulsive speed in your driving.
A thousand dollars in tolls.
I mean, after all,
you are young and postpartum.

Did you notice the floors
of my house need to be swept again?
Or that I've started dropping things—
ballpoint pens, frying pans,
hairs from the length of my comb?
In a vase on the counter, peonies
un-mirth in pink and collapse.

Your husband is gone.
But the baby, what a ladybug,
dimpled buddha with a belly laugh.
I was so sure it would work.
Formula, meaning more
than what the baby drinks.
I let it waft like burnt sage into the corners
of the rooms when I took you all in.
A potent potpourri that sours
in the intestines of the vacuum cleaner.

Check beneath the cushions of the couch.
In the cabinet by the can of bacon grease.
It's gone. I'm talking about hope.
Seeds of it unearthed and eaten
by something wild with a tangled tail.
Mercy, but who left the door open again?
Hurry, now, and go bring me the broom.

When Your Jamaican Grandmother Sings to You

I listen with my eyes.
Your new bones attune to an old song.
Your mouth rounds open.
You are already a choir, angel,
a myriad of assembled voices
wrapped in a pink blanket.

Your grandmother's voice—a port city,
ballsy notes of vendors, shucked fish scales,
thumping boat hulls on a tallawah tide.
Wind in all its lush and leafy affirmations.

We river together,
                she and I,
                        in you.

Our marrows, full of syllables
shushed and braided beneath
the deft fingers of our tribal mothers.
Mine, a blueprint of winter light,
palate of birch and wheat—
milky and spooned in
Am I more visible in this white skin?
Our histories, a different kind of submission.
    We are women, after all.

I want you to know I am listening,
disquieted by your connection.
There's no lullaby in your grandmother's song
of safekeeping. You will be judged and categorized,
little one. Throwing your arms up now
as if they are feathered. Your voice, a wishbone—
an infant stage of mouthed textures, vowels
and consonants gathered and ringing out.

Time Zones

Caretaker, guardian,
    not a label I thought I'd have at this age.
Not for a baby, at any rate.
Already two generations apart,
    I've flown six time zones away
    on an eleven-day journey.

In Norway, everything is electric.
I mean that in terms of transport,
    but also, as in being in another world—
Viking fjords in ice blue,
    glacier-cast mountains that thumb up
      and swallow portions of the sky.
We leave video messages for you
        from overlooks and trains.

I can feel you here—
  your baby cheeks and newly tactile fingers,
    your cloud of black curls.

There is already a chill in the air, but the light is still
long and glowing while we sleep, pale lager in our veins.
    Leaves on the aspen trees going golden.
      They twirl and sputter like windchimes,

channeling current—
    the onset of autumn. Cyclical,
a word that might be used to describe anything,
little one, my namesake back home.

Since I've been gone,
    two teeth have pebbled up to landmark
        another stage of your infancy,
while metamorphic inclines and brightly painted houses
    fly by our windows in gasps.
The horizon, kinetic and thrumming us forward.

Lullaby in Perspective

You and I took the train up the east coast, daughter,
   when you were six months old.
      We rattled across matchstick trellises,
  rivers, hundreds of feet below.

From our small bunker,
   the world was white noise—water
carving stone, trees nodding in silhouette,
   solitary windows squaring with lamplight.

When your hand found my face, you cooed—
   a language, primitive and reciprocal.
      Isn't it curious how we need each other—
beings fashioned of tissue, water, threads
   of nerve cells, elemental rhythms
      in skin that bruises and burns.

Now it is your daughter who needs me
  to lie down beside her so she can sleep.
  Her dark eyes, a palette of shine.

In stratospheres layered above us,
   satellites fidget and bob
     like metallic kites. Jets propel
through air thin with oxygen,
   and navigate latitudes & longitudes,
  trade winds, shorelines and highways.
    Crescent moon

    on the baby's dresser, an electric nightlight
that throws lumens too small to be seen from space,

and from the other side of the door,
 the dog loudly whiffs the length
    of the threshold in between
        as if he could render us whole.
We, who are familiar and necessary,
     an essence in the canyons of his nose.

Nocturnal, the Dark and Squirming

ants that river into your room after midnight.
I can't stay here anymore, is what you tell me.
The ants, sudden and swarming your walls,
your clothes, your bedsheets. A vigil of hunger
hived by day and rampaging at night.
How about some caulk around the windows?
Your father suggests to the landlord.
Genus Camponotus, the scientific name
for what unearths you from your sleep.
My daughter, I know your pillow must house
a hill of them. I imagine the channels being forged.
Cells that hold eggs and larvae and pupae—
images that are viscous and make you retch.
Okay, maybe they're not that bad,
someone will try to tell you in the morning.
Insomniac, a word too long to fit
around the circumference of your coffee cup.
Anxiety is more like it. Look, you say,
pointing to the surfaces of your room—
sunlit and swept clean of crumbs.

Come to Where I Live, She Says

Come to where I live, she says. There are voices cannibalizing each other on the other side of the wall and an effigy in my window—Mother Mary in plaster won at a church raffle.

Come to where I live, she says. The lies I tell you will pool in purple and black across my skin. The man who broke my nose will bail me out of jail, then ask you for the money.

Come to where I live, she says. I'll walk home alone in the dark on the highway after the late shift at the fast-food restaurant. Tomorrow I'll sleep in patterns of kittens that motif my pink sheets. I wonder if my roommates can hear me scream into my pillow.

Come to where I live, she says. I'll have you arrested for trespassing. I won't tell you I'm thinking about dying, and I know how I'll do it. To me, there's nothing worse than a threat. Your agony will be worth my dignity.

Come to where I live, she says. Bring quarters for the laundromat. A demon has poisoned my potted plants. I'm too sad to make it to the door, I've turned to concrete in my bed. A concrete woman with clothes that smell like mold. I might be hungry.

Come to where I live, she says. We'll drink Courvoisier till we float like clouds. Did I tell you it tastes like pears and honeysuckle and the bark of angels hidden in the baseboards? Did I tell you I got my hair braided? Did I tell you I love everyone?

Come to where I live, she says. There are two states of my being. I am sorry and grateful. I haven't returned your calls since Christmas, but I want you to know I love you like the earth from the distance of a kite, a satellite, a comet fevered & orbiting.

Each, a Fossil of Finer Urgencies

Tonight, the stars open with the same
primal blue of dusk. Earth succinct
in its ancient inceptions. A moth
on my windowsill spreads its soft wings—

each, a fossil of finer urgencies. A mask
of eyespots is mirrored across its wingspan.
Never mind nature's penchant for symmetry,
or how the bald sockets became eclipsed

with moon-shaped pupils realistic enough
to startle birds from their hunger.
How does one generation encode the next
with what it will need once uncocooned?

If not a wide-eyed template of iridescence,
or camouflage in motifs of leaf or lichen,
why not a resistance to the heckling lamplight
that will shred those wings by morning?

Namesake

She loves to find the moon,
knows nothing of its shapeshifting,
only of its smeared light on the glass
beneath her small finger pointing up.

Daughter of my daughter—
you, who opened your throat to howl
and lodged the moon there, sharp and lucent.
Mood swings, another name for the phases

of your waxing and waning,
of that persistent incarnation that goes dark
with the collective shadows of us,
our faces furrowed and leaning in.

You'll bring yourself back in increments
of borrowed light. Amber. Gold. Honey,
don't leave without telling us
where to find you. *Defiant*, you say,

praising your daughter's unruly baby curls.
Did you know she is afraid of owls?
Her gray guardian, soother of shadows,
I spoon in lullabies and lamplight
till she believes the night is full of shiny notions—
angel orbs and flickering votives of stars.

Slow down, daughter, slow down.
Sage your bones of yesterday's rum and fury.
Your daughter is at the window tonight.
It's not just the moon she is looking for.

She Who Begat Her Who Begat Her

It sounds like a cadence, the order of us—
    mothers and daughters.
Maybe it's a prayer or a spell. I've known five
generations now. We've risen, sacred
and consecrated from each other's flesh—
a myriad of Venuses heaved out onto the sands.

There's nothing mythological here.
We've traveled a bit, brought in other continents.
Still, we're all firstborn daughters.
Some of us are left-handed,
some of us share the same first name.
None of us has the same eyes,
variations that have gone browner.

The bow in my granddaughter's bottom lip
is something my grandmother called lucky,
meaning an optimist, a girl with a joyful nature.
In the middle, I pivot. My mother alone
in her house, remembers foreign cities,
while the baby, my granddaughter, is trying
to pull herself up, and so is her mother.

We are a shared biology,
conjured from our blood,
rationed for the journey, bits of DNA,
jot and tittle—tiny strokes
inked in the letters of the subtext
that tells our separate stories.

I haven't gone grey yet, but the woman
who cuts my hair says I have a stream of silver
behind each ear. Like a warrioress, she says,
holding a mirror angled at another mirror,
until I see it. Strands like shiny threads.
Maybe it's hereditary, she says.

About the Author

Laura Sobbott Ross has worked as a teacher and a writing coach for Lake County Schools in Central Florida and was named Lake County's inaugural poet laureate. Her poems have been featured on *Verse Daily* and have appeared in *Meridian, 32 Poems, Blackbird, Florida Review,* and elsewhere. She was a finalist for the Art & Letters Poetry Prize and won the Southern Humanities Auburn Witness Poetry Prize. She is the author of six poetry books.

www.ingramcontent.com/pod-product-compliance
Lightning Source LLC
Chambersburg PA
CBHW030917170426
43193CB00009BA/885